SUMMARY

OF THE

Administration

OF THE

INDIAN GOVERNMENT

Owing to the antiquity and rarity of this book, certain pages are regrettably absent, and readability is compromised due to the blurring of the original text. If you possess any insights regarding the availability of these missing sections, kindly inform us. Your assistance is crucial in ensuring the completion of this significant work for the benefit of future generations.

SUMMARY

OF THE

Administration

OF THE

INDIAN GOVERNMENT,

FROM

OCTOBER 1813, to *JANUARY* 1823.

BY THE

MARQUESS OF HASTINGS,

GOVERNOR-GENERAL.

GYAN

Published by

Gyan Publishing House
5, Ansari Road
Daryaganj, New Delhi-110002
Phone: 011-47034999, 9811692060
E-mail: books@gyanbooks.com

Distribution Network
gyanbooks.com
India, USA, Canada, UK, Australia

ISBN: 978-81-212-4932-4 (HB)
First Published, 1824

2nd Impression 2024

Printed at: Gyan Press, Delhi.

SUMMARY OF THE ADMINISTRATION OF THE INDIAN GOVERNMENT
Author: MARQUESS OF HASTINGS

SUMMARY

OF THE

Administration

OF THE

INDIAN GOVERNMENT,

BY THE

MARQUESS OF HASTINGS,

DURING

THE PERIOD THAT HE FILLED THE OFFICE

OF

GOVERNOR GENERAL.

LONDON:
WILLIAM EARLE, BERKELEY SQUARE.

1824.

SUMMARY,

&c. &c.

The solicitude which every one of just feelings must experience to prove his having adequately fulfilled an important trust, ought in my case to be increased by the peculiar nature of the office which I have held. The extent and multiplicity of its functions are little understood at home; and still less are those circumstances comprehended, which called upon me for exertions beyond the ordinary demands of my situation. If those unusual efforts were not necessary, they either risked improvidently the welfare of the Honourable Company, or they were illicit aggressions on weak, unoffending native Powers. It thence behoves me to justify the principle and the prosecution of the measures alluded to. The exposition will be short, because it aims not at submitting any detail of operations. A statement of the ground on which each material determination rested, will enable every one to decide on the equity, as well as prudence of the course adopted; while the general result may answer whether the main object of the Honourable Company's financial prosperity was duly kept in sight, during those complicated transactions. The facts asserted are so supported as not to admit of controversy. Proofs of them are for the most part in the hands of the Court. Where that is not the case, the official vouchers will be found in the Appendix: and it is hoped it will appear, that whatsoever were the advantages attained for the Honourable Company, the interests of our country at large have been simultaneously promoted; the comforts of the Indian population being at the same time signally consulted.

I entered upon the management of affairs at Calcutta, in October 1813. My first view of them was by no means pleasing. The treasuries of the three Presidencies were in so unfurnished a condition, that the insufficiency of funds in them to meet any unusual charges, (and many such menaced us) excited considerable uneasiness. At that period the low credit of the bonds, which had at different times been issued as the securities for monies borrowed, made eventual recourse to a loan seriously discouraging in contemplation. As twelve per cent. discount on the above securities was the regularly calculable rate in the market, when no immediate exigency pressed upon us, the grievous terms to which we must have subscribed for a new supply of that nature, in an hour of alarm could not be disguised to any foresight. Under this embarrassment, an attempt had been made by the preceding government to provide in a partial degree for the anticipated difficulties, by curtailing the annual disbursement, so as to leave a surplus of receipt. What are called the military charges, the provision for all warlike objects, offensive or defensive, had appeared the only head of expenditure in which a saving of efficacious magnitude could be made. The paring knife was thence applied with rather an undiscriminating hand to many of the articles of the military establishment which had till then been deemed indispensable towards a tranquil tenure of the country. As it was matter of simple arithmetical measurement the contemplated surplus was produced; but it was attended with circumstances which had not been taken into reckoning. Let it not be supposed that I am insinuating a censure on an expedient to which the Government was pressingly urged by financial difficulties. The limit within which a reduction of disbursement in the military branch would not entail mischief, was perhaps not to be computed without trial. As it was, experience shewed that hazard had been incurred in a degree quite unapprehended. The saving had principally arisen from a great diminution of our armed force. The operation of such a measure was not confined to the question of sufficiency for eventual defence; nothing would mislead the judgment more than a parallel between the employment of the Indian army, and that of our military at home. The native troops are, in fact, the police of India; the Burkendauzes, or armed attendants of the magistrates, being totally inadequate, if not supported by the regulars. Hence the complication of duties resting upon the soldiery is so great, as that it is rare for even half of a battalion to be found at its head-quarters. Occupation of dependant stations; detachments with treasure, which is in constant transit; escort of stores periodically despatched from Calcutta to the several provinces; charge of convicts working on the roads; custody of prisoners transmitted from different parts for trial before the courts of circuit, and guards over gaols, form a mass of demand which our fullest military complement could barely answer. A great number of those among whom such duties had been divided, could not be dismissed without causing the service to be oppressive to the remainder; but there was a further consequence which rendered the burthen intolerable to the native soldier. This incompetence of strength involved nearly an extinction of those leaves which it had been the custom to grant annually, for a proportion of the men in each regiment to visit their villages: the privation of hope to see his connections occasionally, was insuperably irksome to the Bengal sepoy, usually of high caste. In consequence, very many in each corps solicited discharge from the service. Unless when in the field this indulgence had been uniformly conceded on application, as the individual had received no bounty on entrance; of course there was an aukwardness in refusing what had from practice assumed a color of right, when contest was only secretly anticipated by Government from particulars which it wished not to divulge. So many of those who thus petitioned to quit the service, were veterans approaching the periods of claim to the invalid pension (the great object of the native soldier), that the sacrifice which they desired to make, exhibited unequivocally the deep discontent of the army. I therefore found Government convinced that perseverance in the experiment was too dangerous; and the re-adoption of those military provisions which had been stricken off, would have taken place, even had not another consideration pressed its being done with the utmost speed. The disgust of our native troops was so loudly expressed in all quarters, that the causes of it were universally canvassed, and as such an extraordinary lessening of our military means was ascribed to uncontrollable necessity, the same inferences of our debility were drawn by all the surrounding states. As might have been expected, a tone and procedure altogether novel, had been assumed towards the British Government. There were made over to me, when the reins were placed in my hands, no less than six hostile discussions with native powers, each capable of entailing resort to arms. It was thence obvious, that a beneficial alteration in our pecuniary condition was not to be effected by parting with the sinews of our strength; but by striving to cultivate and render more productive those sources of revenue which we possessed. In the abovementioned number of angry controversies, no advertence is made to the Pindarries. Communication could not be held with those execrable spoilers; yet the atrocity of their character, though it forbad the degradation of negociating with them, could not disparage their inherent force, so as to prevent my regarding them, even at that juncture, as the most serious of the difficulties with which I had to deal. Could the moral call, for suppressing one of the most dreadful scourges that ever afflicted humanity, be set aside, still the task of dispersing an association, whose existence was irreconcileable to our ultimate security, as well as to our more immediate interests, seemed to me not capable of being long postponed. At the same time, I saw the intimacy of connexion between the Pindarries and the Mahrattas, so distinctly, as to be certain that an attempt to destroy the former, must infallibly engage us in war with the whole body of the latter. While the extreme effort was delayed, which our entanglements in other quarters made unavoidable, it was desirable to impose some check upon the plunderers. The year before my arrival, they had ravaged part of our territories; they had carried off an immense booty, with impunity; and they were professedly meditating another invasion. Every military man well comprehends, that defensive frontier stations, though heavily expensive to the state, were absolutely nugatory against a mounted enemy without baggage, following at will, through a vast expanse of country, any line, which the information of the moment might recommend. There was a chance that interposition from Gwalior might cause the

Pindarries to suspend their inroads. It was inappreciable to us, to stop if possible the projected devastation, while we were to be occupied elsewhere; on which account, I proposed a remonstrance to that Court, on the score of the Pindarries being permitted to arrange within the Maharajah's dominions, the preparations for assailing the Honourable Company's provinces. The present unreserved acknowledgement of our supremacy throughout India, will scarcely leave credible the then existence of a relative position, which could occasion my being met in council, by a representation, that a remonstrance of the above nature might be offensive to Scindiah, and that nothing ought to be ventured which could give him umbrage. Such, however, was at that period on either side the estimate of British power.

This introduction, though longer than I could have wished, was necessary to render our circumstances at that crisis accurately intelligible. There was especially a necessity to explain why, when a surplus of revenue had been actually exhibited, it had no permanence. The delusiveness of the principle on which such a surplus had for the moment been obtained, has been disclosed; and it will be understood that we were to seek other supplies, should contests not be avoidable. A large sum is always required to be kept in hand by Government for current purposes; because the revenue from land (the chief article in our income) is not receivable at periods corresponding with the regular disbursements, and is moreover liable to defalcation from the remission allowed in case of bad seasons. Therefore a sum deemed simply adequate to this object cannot be relied upon as a provision for a further contingency. Of the six disputes which I have noticed, four were amicably adjusted; one, in the instance of Rewah, was speedily settled by the storm of a principal fortress, with the menace of a siege to its capital; and the sixth (the contention with Nipaul) remained for decision by arms. A struggle with the latter was unpromising. We were strangely ignorant of the country or its resources; so that, overlooking the augmented abilities latterly furnished by science to a regular army, for surmounting local obstacles, it was a received persuasion that the nature of the mountainous tract which we should have to penetrate, would be as baffling to any exertions of ours, as it had been to all the efforts of many successive Mahommedan sovereigns; no option, however, remained with us. We were not through a point of honour demanding atonement for the wanton invasion of our territories, the brutal massacre of our police man, and the studied cruelty of tying to a tree and shooting to death with arrows the native officer whom we had appointed to preside over the district; though the hopelessness of obtaining from the Government any disavowal of such a complicated outrage, must have made us look to war, even on that ground. But we were at issue with a nation so extravagantly presumptuous respecting its own strength, and so ignorant of our superior means, that the Gorka commissioners had on a former occasion remarked to ours, the futility of debating about a few square miles of territory, since there never could be real peace between the two States, until we should yield to the Gorkas our provinces north of the Ganges, making that river the boundary between us; as Heaven had evidently designed it to be. The conviction that the evil day of contest could not be put off weighed heavily on the minds of functionaries in Calcutta. The possible necessity of withholding an investment was anticipated, and even hinted to the Court of Directors. I endeavoured to allay this anxiety by assurances, that as far as my professional judgment went, the difficulties of mountain warfare were greater on the defensive side, than on that of a well-conducted offensive operation; that I believed myself able to calculate tolerably what expenditure would be entailed by the necessary efforts, estimating the charge much below what they apprehended; and that I could look with confidence to a supply of treasure from a source which they had never contemplated. Soon after my arrival in India, some British officers came to me from the Nawab Vizier Saadat Ali, Sovereign of Oude, bringing to me a representation of the painful and degrading thraldom in which, through gradual, and probably unintended encroachments on his freedom, he was held, inconsistently with the spirit of the treaty between the two States. The system from which he prayed to be released, appeared to me no less repugnant to policy than to equity. On my professing a disposition to correct so objectionable a course, those officers (who had been long in the Nawab Vizier's service) assured me that any persuasion of my having such an inclination would cause Saadat Ali to throw himself upon me with unbounded confidence; and to offer from his immense hoard, the advance of any sum I could want for the enterprise against Nipaul. The gratitude with which such a supply would be felt was professed. While I was on my passage up the Ganges, Saadat Ali unexpectedly died. I found, however, that what had been provisionally agitated by him was perfectly understood by his successor; so that the latter came forward with a spontaneous offer of a crore of rupees, which I declined, as a peishcush or tribute on his accession to the sovereignty of Oude; but accepted as a loan for the Honourable Company. Eight lacks were afterwards added to this sum, in order that the interest at six per cent of the whole might equal the allowances to different branches of the Nawab Vizier's family, for which the guarantee of the British Government had been pledged, and the payment of which without vexatious retardments was secured by the appropriation of the interest to the specific purpose. The sum thus obtained was thrown into the general treasury, whence I looked to draw such portions of it as the demands for the approaching military service might require. My surprise is not to be expressed, when I was shortly after informed from Calcutta, that it had been deemed expedient to employ fifty-four lacks of the sum obtained by me, in discharging an eight per cent. loan; that the remainder was indispensable for current purposes; and that it was hoped I should be able to procure from the Nawab Vizier a further aid for the objects of the war. This took place early in autumn, and the operations against Nepaul could not commence until the middle of November, on which account the Council did not apprehend my being subjected to any sudden inconvenience, through its disposal of the first sum. Luckily I was upon such frank terms with the Nawab Vizier, that I could explain to him fairly my circumstances. He agreed to furnish another crore; so that the Honourable Company was accommodated with above two millions and a half sterling on my simple receipt. Particular details of the war in Nipaul would be superfluous; the terms on which it closed will suffice. That State, instead of flanking, as it had done for nearly six hundred miles, our open frontier or that of the Nawab Vizier, which we were bound to defend, while itself could only be attacked in front, was reduced to about a half of its original extent; remaining with both its flanks exposed to us, through the connexion which we formed with the Rajah to the east, and our possessions of Kemaoun to the west. The richest portion of the territory conquered by us bordered on the dominions of the Nawab Vizier. I arranged the transfer of that track to him, in extinction of the second crore. The charges of the war absorbed fifty-two lacks; forty-eight lacks (£600,000) were consequently left in the treasury a clear gain to the Honourable Company, in addition to the benefit of precluding future annoyance from an insolent neighbour.

While the war was raging in the mountains, my attention was anxiously fixed upon our southern boundaries. I had traced many indications of active communication between States, which had for many years no political intercourse. As I could not then know, what has since transpired, that a wide conspiracy was forming for the expulsion of the British from India, I ascribed the symptoms to vague speculations excited in the native powers, by seeing us engaged in an undertaking where they considered our failure certain. The anticipated exhaustion of our strength in the rash enterprise would present advantages, for the improvement of which they might think it desirable to be prepared; and their several views were to be reciprocally ascertained for the eventual crisis. This spirit, though it did not lead them to immediate action, would naturally prompt them to steps which could not be regarded by us with indifference: in one instance the forecasting disposition of our neighbours shewed an intelligible consistence. An agreement was made between Scindiah and the Rajah of Nagpore, that the forces of both should act under Scindiah, for the reduction of Bhopaul. The very terms of the agreement betrayed the real object; for Bhopaul, when conquered, was to be made over to the Nagpore Rajah. It was obvious that Scindiah only wanted an excuse for bringing the Nagpore troops into junction with those under his command, in which case he would have found himself at the head of a very powerful army. It was not a moment for hesitation. Had Scindiah's forces, which were assembled and ready to march, once entered Bhopaul, shame would have made him risk any extremity, rather than recede upon our intervention. The Nawab of Bhopaul had solicited to be taken under British protection. I was at that time on Scindiah's frontiers, my escort being composed of one weak battalion of native infantry, a troop of the body guard, and a squadron of native cavalry. In three weeks I could not have assembled three thousand men, all our disposable force being employed against Nepaul. But the case called for decision; and I directed the resident at Scindiah's court to request that his Highness would forbear any aggression upon Bhopaul, as that state had become an ally to our Government. I desired that this communication should be made in the most conciliatory tone; and that the resident would not report to me the violent language with which it would probably be met by Scindiah, so that there might be no affront to discuss. There was seemingly hardihood in this procedure; but there was essentially none. Supposing Scindiah predetermined to go all lengths, any provocation from my message was of no moment. If he were only trying his ground, and taking steps towards rendering a remoter decision more secure, the unexpected check might make him pause; and the gain of time was every thing to me, when I was disciplining recruits in all quarters for the augmentation of our force. Scindiah, as was unofficially reported to me, received the intimation with all the vehemence of language which I had expected. But notwithstanding his declaration, that he should follow his own course, his troops did not move, and the project against Bhopaul was silently abandoned. The Maharajah must have been influenced by the supposition, that the confidence of my procedure, and the apparent carelessness of my progress along the frontier with so slender an accompaniment, arose from my possession of means which he could not calculate.

The resident in a later day made a merit with Scindiah of having suppressed, in his report to me, the offensive tone which he had used; and his Highness acknowledged the obligation. The circumstances which I have detailed will give a useful insight into the doubtful terms on which we then stood with the neighbouring states. Whether positive engagements had secretly taken place among them was uncertain: it was at all events clear that they looked to a possible junction, when they might pursue a common object necessarily unfavourable to us. When Ummar Sing Kappa and Runjour Sing, generals of the Gorkhas, had surrendered themselves, they could not be brought to believe that the Mahrattas were not actually in the field against us, though neither of them would assign a reason for the supposition. As they had severally professed the persuasion when they could not have had communication, it was evident that each of them must have had knowledge of proposals for co-operation made by the Mahrattas to his court. Early in 1816 an event occurred, seemingly unconnected with the suspicious indications which were fixing our attention in other parts; but really deriving great moment from reference to those symptoms. Scindiah had in 1808 given up to us, by treaty, extensive possessions in the Doab, or tract contained between the Ganges and the Jumna. Those lands were inhabited by Jauts, a hardy and warlike tribe. This ceded territory was divided into several petty districts, each under a Talochdar, corresponding to the Zemindar of the lower provinces. From the exposure of the country to frequent invasion from predatory cavalry, the distant sovereign, who had not management enough in his dominions to shield his detached provinces from such inroads, was forced to consult his own interest as to pecuniary returns, by allowing these Talochdars to have fortified residencies, where the treasure was lodged, as collected for ultimate remittance to the treasury of Gwalior. The permission for maintaining a fortress necessarily included a garrison, which, from vanity or views of depredation, had, in every instance, been carried far beyond what the duties of the place required. It is probable that these Talochdars had been looking forward to a time when they might cast off their allegiance to the Mahratta rule, and render themselves independent chiefs of little principalities. Their assiduity in strengthening their fortresses, may be ascribed to the anticipation of such a favourable hour: they were encouraged in this speculation by the circumstance that the Rajah of Bhurtpore, whose power was rated high from his successful resistance to the British, had affinity with the principal families. He and his people are Jauts. In practice, the situation of the Talochdar, under the Mahrattas, united the characters of a middle man and the manager of an absentee's estate in Ireland, with whatsoever degree of authority over the peasantry he thought proper to usurp; knowing that his Government would never be at the trouble of calling him to an account. The most populous and productive of the districts were under the superintendance of Dya Ram; an active, ambitious man, whose preponderance in the tribe was supported by amassed riches, as well as personal energy. Calculating on a future opportunity for establishing sway over the rest, he employed himself sedulously in perfecting his fortress of Hattrass, which he had originally found of great strength, and in keeping up the discipline of a well-organized force. When this territory was surrendered to the British Government, though our judicial administration was declaredly introduced into it, considerations, deemed politic, led us to withhold a strict enforcement of our regulations. For obvious reasons, we had never heretofore suffered a strong hold to be possessed by an individual in our provinces. On this occasion we deviated from our caution, and did not insist on the immediate demolition of the fortresses, in the territory transferred to us. I have understood it was conceived, that when the Talochdars should find themselves efficiently protected from external violence, they would gladly forego the expense of providing for their own security, and would without repugnance dismantle their forts, which they were told would ultimately be required of them. Perhaps there was an error in supposing, that after having been continued for a time in the enjoyment of what flattered their pride, they would feel less the sacrifice of the distinction. As it was, they evidently made common cause in a plan for evading that humiliation. They encouraged each other in the resolution, by promises of reciprocal aid; and from the confidence thus inspired, they gradually assumed an undisguised air of pretension to be on the footing of mere tributary dependance. This disposition became more marked and overt at the period to which I have before alluded, when the ruin of our Government had become matter of general belief, and manifold trespasses on our authority were impudently committed by these Talochdars. Our occupation with Nepaul constrained us to shut our eyes as much as might be, on these encroachments; an impunity which naturally invited more determined steps. As soon as our hands were free, it became necessary to notice those irregularities, therefore it was signified to the Talochdars, that any repetition of them would meet with decided chastisement. The intimation was wholly disregarded. At length, the Members of Council unanimously represented to me (I having then returned to Calcutta from the Upper Provinces), a daring defiance of our legitimate jurisdiction by

Dya Ram, who had seized and kept in irons within his fortress several of our police officers, for arresting a robber within his District; and who had, moreover, caused a party of his troops to confine for twenty-four hours in a village, the Judge and Magistrate of the Zillah, containing these Talooks. This was communicated to me with anxiety, because the supposed strength of Hattrass made it appear awkward to undertake the correction of Dya Ram. Punishment of the substantive offence was of itself imperiously demanded; but the urgent expedience of bringing the whole body of those Jauts definitively into regular submission as subjects, was as strikingly visible. As I had not however before learned the particulars to which the Members of Council referred, I answered, that if they would lay before me such a case, sustained by due evidence, as should prove Dya Ram to have incurred the penalty, Hattrass should be reduced; an operation which I pledged myself to them, should not require eight and forty hours for its completion, after the batteries had opened against the place. When I was in the upper country, it had, of course, been my duty to obtain minute information respecting every fortress with which any chance might bring us into contact; and I had procured the requisite knowledge of Hattrass among the rest. That fort had the reputation of being impregnable, which silly persuasion had betrayed Dya Ram into his contumacious outrages. According to the mode of attack which the natives had been accustomed to see practised by us, Hattrass might, indeed, appear formidable to meddle with. A ditch of 120 feet wide, and 85 deep, surrounded a work, which, in triple tier of defences, exhibited a provision for contesting the place inch by inch, after the silencing of its artillery, and the making a practicable breach, should bring the besieger to the point of storming. Luckily, science has laid down procedures for avoiding the necessity of hazarding a disadvantageous assault; one of my earliest military cares on arriving in India, had been to satisfy myself why we had made so comparatively unfavourable a display in sieges. The details at once unfolded the cause; it is well known that nothing can be more insignificant than shells thrown with long intervals; and we never brought forward more than four or five mortars where we undertook the capture of a fortified place. Hence, the bombardment was futile, so that at last the issue was to be staked on mounting a breach, and fighting hand to hand with a soldiery skilful, as well as gallant, in defending the prepared intrenchments. This was not the oversight of the Bengal Artillery officers, for no men can be better instructed in the theory, or more capable in the practice of their profession than they are. It was imputable to a false economy on the part of the Government: the outlay, in providing for the transportation of mortars, shells, and platforms, in due quantity, would certainly have been considerable; and it was on that account forborne: the miserable carriages of the country, hired for the purpose, where a military exertion was contemplated, were utterly unequal to the service, and constantly failed under the unusual weight in the deep roads through which they had to pass. Therefore, we never sat down before a place of real strength, furnished with the means which a proper calculation would have allotted for its reduction. Sensible of this injurious deficiency, I had with the utmost diligence instituted a transport train; and it was in reliance on its efficiency that I assured the Council of the short resistance which Hattrass should offer. Expedition no less than secrecy was important, to prevent any interventions which might trouble us in the undertaking; and notwithstanding that the advance of the troops was so rapid, that Dya Ram had information of their approach only two days before Hattrass was actually invested, forty-two mortars kept pace with the march of the force; and from the incessant shower of bombs the garrison was unable to persist in defending the place more than fifteen hours. The body of troops employed was of such strength, that no sudden assemblage could venture to face it, while the speedy effectuation of the object left no time for interference from remoter quarters. Thus, uninterrupted, the officer commanding it, according to his orders, summoned successively the other fortresses of the Jauts. Terrified by the fate of Hattrass, all of them to the number of eleven, some very strong, surrendered without resistance: the works were every where razed, and the troops attached to them were disbanded, except a few armed attendants allowed for security to the household of each of the Talochdars, in a country not yet brought into habitual regularity. The Talochdars were indemnified for the cannon and arms of which they were dispossessed, being further maintained in as much convenience as was consistent with the laws of the British Government. Those terms, with an oblivion of his past misdeeds, had been offered to Dya Ram on the first appearance of the troops before Hattrass, and had been rejected by him; therefore, his lands were declared forfeited. Thus was effected, at a critical juncture, an object pressingly incumbent in itself; I mean the assimilation of those Jaut communities to the orderly condition of our other native subjects: but of enhanced importance to their otherwise possible insurrection in the centre of our possessions when our force was engaged elsewhere; whether that insurrection should arise from secret preconcert with powers leagued against us, or be stimulated by accidental temptations. The politics of the Rajah of Bhurtpore, would be seriously influenced by deprivation of an eventual support from his tribe; and every Prince in India must have felt a diminution of the confidence with which he would have opposed us when the fall of Hattrass dissipated his trust in fortifications. It is not altogether irrelevant to add, that an annual saving, by no means insignificant, has arisen from the transport trains being employed during the peace in collateral services under the Commissariat department, of which I constituted it a branch.

While the fermentation perceivable in the Mahratta States could be ascribed to the tempting prospect of a particular opportunity, there was the hope that, when all chance of such an opening had passed away, the machinations would subside. Many symptoms concurring to prove that this was not the case, the conclusion was irresistible, that a more defined and methodized understanding of a tenor hostile to us, had been established, at least among the powers upholding the predatory system in Central India. Their success in seducing other Native States into pledges for acting in concert, could not be judged, as I have mentioned that our discoveries had then gone no further than the ascertaining that there were frequent missions, conducted with great stealth, between powers not in prior habits of communication. The symptoms might be fallible; yet common caution required that the no longer postponable enterprize of extirpating the Pindarries, who had again mercilessly laid waste our territories, should embrace a provision for encountering the widest combination among the Native States. Supposing their confederacy to be actually established, and that I failed in the project I had formed for rendering the collection of their forces impracticable, I was to look to coping with little less than three hundred thousand men in the field. It was a formidable struggle to incur; such indeed as it would have been irreconcileable to my duty towards my employers to have risked, had the hazard been avoidable. I think, however, that no one who considers the circumstances will regard it as having been adventured wilfully or inexpediently; I refer not to the fortunate issue, which is always a doubtful criterion of policy. I desire my position to be fairly examined. If it be evident that the contest, whether it should originate in a conspiracy of the Native Sovereigns, or in the support given by the Mahratta States and Ameer Khan to the Pindarries, was not ultimately to be avoided, the question was only when and how it might be entered on with the best chances of success ; and I believe I decided as was imperiously demanded by the interests with which I stood entrusted. I calculated that by celerity of movement on our part, the ill-disposed might be incapacitated from attempting the opposition which they meditated ; and any appearance of our proceeding upon unconfirmed suspicions would be far counterbalanced by their escape from being involved in the destruction of the Pindarries ; still more as the measures held in view promised them their share in the anticipated improvement of condition throughout Central India. Before however our troops were put in motion, our informations respecting the concerted attack upon the British possessions were distinct and incontrovertible.

From Cawnpore, whither I had proceeded, I notified to the Council at Calcutta my purpose of framing the campaign consonantly to the above computation. What I contemplated was the pushing forward unexpectedly several divisions, which should occupy positions opposing insuperable obstacles to the junction of the army of any State with that of another; even subjecting to extreme peril any Sovereign's attempt to assemble the dispersed corps of his forces within his own dominions, should we see cause to forbid it. The success of the plan depended on the secrecy with which the preparations could be made, the proper choice of the points to be seized, and the speed with which we should reach the designated stations. I speak relatively to the troops which were to penetrate from the North; for the advance of those from the South, destined to act against the Pindarries, could not be concealed. The formation of my magazines of grain on the frontier was fortunately disguised by a bad harvest in that quarter, which furnished the excuse for transportation of corn thither, as if it were a provision for the inhabitants against eventual dearth. In all other respects the arrangements were so admirably conducted by the few public functionaries confidentially entrusted with them, that not a suspicion of any intended stir was afloat. In the most distant battalion destined for the service there was not a surmise of impending movement above five or six days previous to its being actually in march. The suddenness with which we occupied the heart of the inimical countries, added to the efficiency of the means employed, caused all the essential parts of the business to be finished completely to my wish in hardly more than three months; so that I was enabled almost immediately after that period to send back to their cantonments that part of the force the most chargeable in the field, the European troops. The vast scale of the operations could not but be attended with great expense; it was from their short duration that, when the war charges came to be wound up, the amount for the six divisions of the Bengal troops brought forward on the occasion did not reach thirty-five lacks of Sonaut rupees, or about thirty-three and a half of Sicca, that is £417,000.* When the charge for the troops periodically and unavailingly moved forward from the Madras presidency, to cover the country south of the Nerbudda from the Pindarries, is considered, and the heavy loss of revenue

* Appendix A.

from the devastations committed by those wretches is taken into account; it may be thought a thrifty expenditure which, at such a rate, once for all put an end to that annual tax upon our finances. In that expenditure is included not only every kind of disbursement usually connected with troops, beyond what would have been required for them had they remained in quarters, but one arising out of the special circumstances. While every exaction for provisions and forage was strictly forborne in the neutral or feudatory countries through which we passed, compensation was made for the damage done by encamping the troops, even for a night, where the ground was under crop, as was almost invariably the case. The injury was estimated between the Chief Commissariat Officer and the principal men of the villages concerned; and the compensation agreed on by them was paid on the spot in ready money. This measure, besides its essential justice, had the object of manifesting to the natives the equity of the British Government, and of inducing such petty independent communities as had not already relations with us to obtain our protection, by voluntarily soliciting to be taken under our paramountship. The expectation did not deceive us: all those little territories, which had till then remained unattached, ranged themselves under our banners. Among other chiefs, the Rajah of Tihree, when he presented his nuzzer in token of plighted fealty, desired me to understand that it was the first time that state had acknowledged the supremacy of another, all the efforts of the Moghul Emperors to subdue it having proved abortive. We were not at the time in the Tihree territories, nor were we likely to enter them, therefore the conduct of the Rajah could only spring from an impression which must be flattering for our country.

The economy of making our exertion so powerful, will be still better comprehended, from a further particular. Trimbuckjee Danglia, the favourite and confidential instrument of the Peishwa, was the immediate agent in the murder of the Guyckwar's minister. Gungudri Shastree, the person in question, had been earnestly invited to Poonah by the Pieshwa, for the ostensible purpose of settling accounts which were afloat between the two states, but with the real object of gaining the minister to seduce his sovereign into the confederacy against us. The Guyckwar, from some doubt of the Pieshwa, would not suffer his minister to repair to Poonah, unless the British Government would be answerable for his safety; and we pledged ourselves to that prince accordingly, not merely in compliance with the solicitation of the Peishwa, but because we were anxious that counter claims between the two states, which had given us such trouble, should be finally adjusted. That a Bramin of the highest cast, first minister of an independent Prince, and invested with a public commission by his Sovereign, should stand in any risk, appeared incredible: therefore our guarantee was unhesitatingly given. When the Pieshwa found, that the minister was proof against all temptation, and refused absolutely to betray his master into a scheme, which the minister thought would entail his destruction, his Highness determined to make away with such an obstacle to his views, in the hope that the office of his minister might be filled by some more manageable individual. Gangudri Shastree was barbarously assassinated, on his way back from a devotional ceremony by night, in the temple, whither he had gone, upon repeated entreaties from Trimbuckjee Danglia, after having previously excused himself on the score of indisposition. The Peishwa was apprized, that his participation in the crime was minutely known to us, but that, to save his credit, the guilt should be thrown on the special perpetrator, Trimbuckjee Danglia, who must be delivered up to us, in atonement for the outrage offered to our plighted security. Trimbuckjee was put into our hands accordingly. To conciliate the Peishwa, it was promised to his Highness that his favourite should not be proceeded against capitally, but be merely kept in confinement as a state prisoner. Trimbuckjee, having made his escape from a fortress, where he was negligently guarded, was afterwards taken in the field, speedily subsequent to the Peishwa's surrender. Regarding the game as irretrievably lost, he thought concealment useless, and indulged that boast of a nearly accomplished design, with which persons often console themselves under failure. He unfolded that, from early in 1814, the Peishwa had been busied in organizing a general confederacy of native powers, for the purpose of driving the British out of India, and heaverred, that we were only by three or four months too quick upon them, or we should have found them the assailants, in which case the issue might have been very different. Certainly had Scindiah, by much the most powerful of the native Princes, been in the field at the head of his assembled veteran troops, with the fine and well manned artillery which he possessed, time as well as encouragement would have been afforded to the other confederate powers, for resorting to arms in so many quarters, as must have made our movements cautious, and consequently protracted, under heavy expense.

The incurrence of such circumstances was, at all events, to be risked by us, since, I repeat, it was not a matter of option, whether the extinction of an evil so intolerable as the ravages of the Pindarries should be undertaken.

It has been said, however, that confident expectation had been entertained of achieving the main purpose, while every hostile speculation of the native Sovereigns would be repressed, by our sudden pre-occupation of particular positions: and this calculation applied in a more special degree to Scindiah. Residing at Gwalior, he was in the heart of the richest part of his dominions: but independently of the objection that those provinces were separated from our territory only by the Jumna, there was a military defect in the situation to which it must be supposed the Maha Rajah had never adverted. About twenty miles south of Gwalior, a ridge of very abrupt hills, covered with the tangled wood peculiar to India, extends from the little Sinde to the Chumbal, which rivers form the flank boundaries of the Gwalior district and its dependencies. There are but two routes by which carriages, and perhaps cavalry, can pass that chain; one along the little Sinde, and another not far from the Chumbal: by my seizing, with the centre division, a position which would bar any movement along the little Sinde, and placing M. General Donkin's division at the back of the other pass, Scindiah was reduced to the dilemma of subscribing the treaty which I offered to him, or of crossing the hills through bye paths, attended by the few followers who might be able to accompany him, sacrificing his splendid train of artillery (above one hundred brass guns), with all its appendages, and abandoning at once to us his most valuable possessions. The terms imposed upon him were, essentially unqualified submission, though so coloured as to avoid making him feel public humiliation. Their intrinsic rigour will not be thought overstrained or inequitable, when it is observed, that I had ascertained the Maharajah's having promised the Pindarries decisive assistance; and that I had intercepted the secret correspondence, through which he was instigating the Nepaulese to attack us. Nothing, in short, but my persuasion, that the maintenance of the existing governments in Central India, and the making them our instruments and sureties for preserving the future tranquillity of the country, would have dictated the forbearance manifested, under the reiterated perfidies of that Prince. He closed with the proffered conditions, and was saved by the acquiescence. The advantage to us was, that resistance in any other quarter could be only a transient ebullition. To the more distant states, this non-appearance of a formidable force, with which they were to co-operate, was absolute incapacitation from effort. In my way back to Calcutta, in July 1818, I received a rescript, brought by an envoy from the Birman monarch, whom we incorrectly call King of Ava, from one of the great divisions of his empire. The purport of this curious paper was, a requisition for our immediate surrender of all the provinces east of the Banghautty, even including Moorshadabad, with a menace, that should the demand not be obeyed, he would lay waste our territories with fire and sword. His projected hostility was evidently a measure concerted with the Mahrattas; and during the rainy season, when the overflowing of the rivers renders the march of troops impracticable, his Majesty conceived, that by advancing a title, however extravagant, to those provinces, he should have an ostensible ground for invading a state, with which otherwise he had no quarrel. I sent back the envoy, with an intimation, that the answer should be conveyed through another channel. He had come from the court through the northern Birman provinces. The answer was dispatched by sea to the Viceroy of Arracan, residing at the port of Rangoon, in the central division, for transmission to his sovereign. It expressed that I was too well acquainted with his Majesty's wisdom, to be the dupe of the gross forgery attempted to be palmed upon me; wherefore I sent to him the document fabricated in his august name, and trusted that he would subject to condign punishment the persons who had so profligately endeavoured to sow dissension between two powers reciprocally interested to cultivate amity. By this procedure I evaded the necessity of noticing an insolent step, foreseeing that his Birman Majesty would be thoroughly glad of the excuse to remain quiet, when he learned his secret allies had been subdued. That information he received at the same time with my letter; all further discussion or explanation being forborne, the former amicable intercourse continued without change. The circumstance will shew the extent to which the negociations of the Mahrattas had gone, exhibiting also the advantage of using exertions so decisive, as should not leave time for distant enemies to come forward.

The former treaty with Scindiah, which I had declared annulled on the proof of his hostile practices, contained an article equally discreditable and embarrassing. We were bound by it to have no correspondence with the Rajpoot States, and were thence debarred from granting to them that protection, which they offered to repay by cooperating for the suppression of the Pindarries. Emancipated from so injurious a shackle, I received all those States as feudatory to the British Government; though each possessed considerable force, their reciprocal estrangements (proceeding chiefly from punctilious and hereditary quarrels between the neighbouring princes) prevented their ever forming any union. They were consequently plundered for a succession of years, not only by the Pindarries, but by the armies of Ameer Khan, of Scindiah, and of Holkar. Devastation had become so familiar to the eyes of the rulers of these countries, that they viewed almost with indifference the oppression exercised over the ryots, or cultivators of the soil, by the troops which garrisoned their fortresses, or were maintained about the sovereign's person. The connexion which they now formed with us, secured them against outrage from without; while a main stipulation on our part was, that their own troops should be subjected to such a system of regularity as would insure the property and domestic quiet of the villager, or entail upon the aggressor an immediate exemplary punishment. The further obligations under which the chieftains placed themselves, were to refer all differences among them to the British Government; to keep a well-equipped contingent in readiness for any call from us; and to employ that soldiery, in the mean time, to crush within their respective states any petty predatory gangs, which might become a nucleus for future mischief. These arrangements, rendered efficacious by very simple measures, adopted on our recommendation, produced to the sovereigns, as well as to the subjects throughout these populous regions, a comfort to which every British individual who has traversed that part of India will bear witness. A more formal testimony is on record. When General Sir D. Ochterlony was to quit Delhi, in order to assume the superintendence of our relations with the Rajpoot

States, he was directed to make an extensive tour through these territories, in order that he might inform the Government at Calcutta what had really been the practical result of our endeavours to ameliorate their condition. A copy of his account is annexed to this document. The nature of the statement admits no loose representation; it is an official report, to the accuracy of which the character of the officer is pledged.*

The campaign closed with our having acquired undisputed sway over every portion of India: the States which had not professedly subscribed to our sovereignty (Gwalior and Bhurtpore) being in truth thence the more entirely subjected to our pleasure, since they were unable to hesitate compliance with any suggestion: while our interference, on whatever plea of public necessity, would not be limited by those reservations which we had defined in favour of the feudatory sovereigns. This advantage for the Honourable Company was greatly enhanced by its having been attained at a price of blood and treasure, short

* Appendix.

of all probability, when the operations were on so vast a scale, that some of the corps, directed to a common centre and object, had been moved from stations distant not less than twelve hundred miles from each other. The dissipation of a serious conspiracy, and the uniting almost every native power with our interests, were still not the only grounds of satisfaction. The important degree in which, as represented by Sir D. Ochterlony, the people of the Rajpoot States, amounting to some millions, were benefited by the procedure of the British Government, will excite lively gratification. That population, however, formed but a part of the immense mass rescued from misery; a lighter term cannot well be used for the condition of those who had been exposed to the ravages of the Pindarries. When it is recollected that the association in question consisted of above thirty thousand mounted men, all professedly subsisting upon plunder, the extent of theatre necessary to furnish an adequate prey may be well conceived. The whole of the Nizam's subjects, as well as the inhabitants of the northern circars of the Madras Presidency, were constantly exposed to devastation. It was not rapine alone, but unexampled barbarity, that marked the course of the spoilers. Their violation of the women, with circumstances of peculiar indignity, which made multitudes of the victims throw themselves into wells, or burn themselves together in straw huts, was invariable; and they subjected the male villagers to refined tortures, in order to exact disclosures where their little hoards of money were buried. From this scourge, the territories to which I have alluded were freed by the annihilation of the Pindarries; and the value of the relief was manifested by the speedy re-occupation and cultivation of extensive districts in the Nizam's dominion, which had for some years lain deserted by the former inhabitants. The extremity of despair, alone capable of making Hindoos abandon their native seats, will be intelligible to all acquainted with India. Had it not been for the timely interposition, large tracts in the Company's provinces would have been similarly depopulated.

A security from external violence was not the only boon which the body of the inhabitants throughout Central India received from the British Government. The anarchy existing in the States, now become feudatory, not only furnished just pretension for recommending arrangements, but made the Chiefs unfeignedly resort to us for aid in fixing the fundamental rules of their government. Confined to their capitals, as they had nearly been for years, through the fear of being cut off by some predatory leader, or by some of their own refractory vassals, they were conscious of inability to restore order in their disorganized dominions; and they frankly invited advice, which, according to my directions, was in every case so respectfully tendered by the British agent, as not to hazard a wound to pride. Thence it was easy, where no acknowledged usages stood in the way, to establish principles between the sovereign and the subject advantageous to both, giving to those principles a defined line of practical application, a departure from which would afford to either party a right of claiming the intervention of our paramount power.

While the sovereign had his legitimate authority and his due revenue insured to him, the subject was protected against illicit exaction or tyrannical outrage. The main danger to this compact lay with the great vassals. They however were unequivocally apprized that any infraction on their part of the promulgated regulations of the State would be immediately chastised by a British force; so that they had not to reckon on the weakness of their sovereign for impunity in any unconstitutional combination. This could not be construed by them as an empty menace: a striking example had been displayed to them; two chiefs dependant on Scindiah, confiding in the strength of the fortresses held by them within his dominions, had disclaimed obedience to him, and remained contumacious, though summoned by us to submit themselves to their sovereign. As a body of our troops were in the neighbourhood, I caused each of the fortresses to be besieged, and as soon as they were surrendered, I put them into the hands of the Maharajah without any demand for the expenses of their reduction. I was guided by two considerations: first, that chiefs destitute of revenue could not maintain garrisons without a license to their men for plundering, which would renew the system I had been eradicating. Secondly, that Scindiah might, from their unchecked insubordination, pretend equal inability to controul others of his vassals; thereby escaping the responsibility which I meant to fix upon him for the maintenance of tranquillity. The measure evinced so clearly the sincerity of our intention to uphold the Maharajah's Government, that it won him to decided reliance upon us, and induced him to meet unhesitatingly many propositions relative to general convenience, which he would otherwise have regarded with jealousy. In particular, I obtained his acquiescence to the keeping up for a further time the contingent of five thousand horse, paid by him, but subject to our requisition and direction. This force he had been bound by an article of the treaty to furnish towards the extirpation of the Pindarries. One of the Company's officers was attached to this corps, under the semblance of securing that its numbers and efficiency should answer to the terms of the engagement; but the Sirdar ostensibly commanding that body, left, with his master's assent, the complete guidance of it in the field to the British officer. Scindiah had evaded producing this contingent until after the destruction of the Pindarries. To compensate for such a delay, which I affected to consider as accidental, I pressed that the corps should be employed in extinguishing certain mischievous associations in Scindiah's territories. The description applied not only to some bands of avowed robbers, but to a particular class denominated Thugs. This nefarious fraternity, amounting, by the first information, to above a thousand individuals, was scattered through different villages often remote from each other; yet they pursued with a species of concert, their avocation. This was the making excursions to distant districts, where, under the appearance of journeying along the high roads, they endeavoured to associate themselves with travellers, by either obtaining leave to accompany them as if for protection, or, when that permission was refused, keeping near them on the same pretext. Their business was to seek an opportunity of murdering the travellers when asleep or off their guard. In this, three or four could combine without having given suspicion of their connection. Though personally unacquainted, they had signs and tokens by which each recognized the other as of the brotherhood; and their object being understood, without the necessity of verbal communication, they shunned all speech with each other till the utterance of a mystical term or two announced the favourable moment, and claimed common effort. Scindiah's tolerance of an evil so perfectly ascertained, merely because the assassinations were seldom committed within his own dominions, may afford a tolerable notion of the vitiation of society in Central India before this late convulsion. There is reason to believe that by this time the pest in question has been rooted out; which, with the suppression of some bodies of horsemen under military adventurers (a service completely achieved by the contingent), will be no less a benefit to Scindiah's own Government, than to adjacent countries. These changes having been effected, no excuse remained with Scindiah why he should not be answerable for any aggressions suffered by his neighbours from parties assembled within his territories. To counterbalance the bond thus imposed upon him, he received signal advantages. It is true he was hemmed round by States leagued with each other and with us; so that, still possessing considerable military means, he could not undertake a war without entailing destruction on himself. But he was incomparably more master over his own Sirdars or leaders of divisions, than he had ever before been: since, if dismissed from his service, they could not debauch the troops which they commanded through the confidence of supporting them by the plunder of other countries; and he had gained materially in point of revenue, both as to the amount and as to the certainty of receipt. A number of insulated patches in Malwa, forming a very considerable aggregate, had belonged to the Peishwa, and by right of conquest devolved to us. Few of these small possessions could be annexed to territories which we meant to retain. Such of these as were contiguous to States, where it was our interest to give additional strength, were gratuitously transferred to those Governments. Where any of these lay between the body of Scindiah's dominions, and some detached district of his, so that by the cession we could connect those territories, we made over our right to the Maharajah by exchanges which were always extraordinarily profitable to him. It was highly gratifying to me, that in this mode I was enabled to bestow on the Nawab of Bhopaul, a splendid reward for the liberality with which he had sold all his jewels to maintain troops in aid of our exertions. The fortress and territory of Islam Nuggur had been the original possession of his family. In the lifetime of his father, Scindiah's predecessor had obtained it through the treachery of the officer to whom it was entrusted; and the strength of the fortress rendered hopeless any endeavour to regain it by siege. This possession, widely separated from the territories of Gwalior, we acquired from Scindiah by giving him in exchange, districts greatly superior in value, as well as adjoining his own dominions; and then we conferred it on the Nawab of Bhopaul, as a free gift to recompense his gallant manifestation of gratitude for the protection his country had received in the crisis of the Nepaul war. The Honourable Company will, no doubt, approve the policy of such an exhibited proof, that attachment to their Government was an advantageous course. In other instances, the exchange was merely territory for territory. Many of the neighbouring States acknowledged tribute as due from them to the Maharajah of Gwalior. It had been a *black mail*, by which they purchased their exemption, ill observed, from predatory incursions. Length of usage had, however, given these payments a colour of right. I desired to extinguish them, that Scindiah might not have a motive or plea for regular communication with these Governments; and I proposed to him that he should accept land in lieu of them, where I could allot to him any tract contiguous to his old possessions. This was agreed upon with large amount of surplus, of yearly income, to him in each exchange; and where the annihilation of the tribute could not be managed on these terms, it was settled that we should regularly pay the sums to Scindiah as they became due, on his transfer of the tributary claim to us. This is noticed, not merely as explaining the precautions taken by us for the future quiet of Central India; but also for the purpose of introducing mention of a circumstance so descriptive of Mahratta principles as to shew the impossibility of reckoning upon tranquillity in India with a less complete revolution than what we effected. Scindiah's Minister appearing not wholly satisfied with the arrangement to which the Maharajah had subscribed, it was represented to him that the gain was unquestionable, since where his Sovereign had received land, there was a considerable accession of territory as well as a great increase of income, beyond the rate of the tribute; while, in the other cases, Scindiah never could have levied the tribute for which we had agreed to furnish the composition, his marching troops through the States dependant on us being interdicted: "True," replied the Minister, "there is a visible immediate profit; but then there is loss of an advantage which we Mahrattas think inestimable, that of having a finger in every man's dish."

All the vices of administration which reigned in Scindiah's dominions, existed no less rootedly within the Poonah State, and that of Nagpore. The population, therefore, in each of those States, as likewise in Holkar's territory, was extraordinarily benefited by the issue of the contest. In the districts which were retained for the Honourable Company, the regular equity of our rule superseded the capricious oppression of the antecedent sway. But even in the dominions restored to the native Princes, our example and advice established a tone of Government altogether unknown before. The general view of policy embraced by us, had been to uphold as much as possible the ancient authorities where we could prevent their being hereafter dangerous: and our principle was to confirm titles as we had found them, without admitting retrospects which could never be satisfactorily determined. One obvious exception to this plan presented itself. The Peishwa Bajee Rao could never be trusted, after his original perfidy in unprovokedly forming a wide conspiracy for the extirpation of the British; and after his subsequent attempt to overwhelm and massacre the British Resident stationed at his court under the pledge of his protection. This criminality of Bajee Rao's was aggravated by the murder in cold blood of British officers who were travelling in his dominions, without suspicion of impending rupture. A more imperious consideration, however, presented itself: we had experienced in the conduct of Toolsye Bhye (the Regent of Holkar's State), and in that of Appa Saheb, Rajah of Nagpore, that no acts of personal kindness, no obligations of plighted faith, no conviction of almost inevitable ruin, could weigh with Mahratta chiefs against the professed bond of obedience to the head of their tribe. It was evident that were such an ostensible superiority to be revived, any compact with Mahratta princes must be nugatory towards the future tranquillity of India. It was indispensable to divorce those sovereigns from acknowledged community of interest. To have put the Sattara family in possession of the Poonah dominions, would have been to create a new leader of the Mahratta confederacy, in whom would have rested all that influence which we had found capable of being so dangerously exerted against us. It was matter of the clearest self-defence, not to resuscitate such a power; Bajee Rao's dominions were therefore declared forfeited. The profligacy of his conduct towards us justly merited that punishment. At the time, however, of his surrender, he had bargained that he should not be kept in close confinement; and that he should have a handsome allowance for his support. These stipulations had been construed with a liberality due to his former eminence. He resides at a station on the Ganges fixed upon by himself, under the sole restriction that he shall not move thence without the assent of the British Government; a limitation so little embarrassing to him in practice, that he has been repeatedly permitted to visit places at which he wished to offer his devotions, though the distance might amount to two hundred miles. In these progresses he has received from every military post, the salutes and attentions customary towards a prince. On his marches, and at his residence, he is surrounded by his own guards, amounting to about four hundred horse and foot; among whom he administers justice in all cases not capital. Beyond his allowance of one hundred thousand pounds yearly, he is in possession of several camel loads of treasure which have never been examined, so that he and his two wives can display any degree of splendour they may wish to exhibit. In short, his situation is as dignified as it can be made, consistently with our security and with the necessary superintendence of a commissioner, who observes towards him every exhibition of respect. His brother Chimnajee resides at Benares on a more moderate, but still generous stipend. To the Sattara Rajah an independent territory has been assigned out of the late Peishwa's possessions. It yields a large revenue, competent to the maintenance of considerable pomp; an extraordinary change of condition for one who used to be kept in strict custody, with a knowledge that the guards set over him had Bajee Rao's orders to put him and his family to death, on any probability of his being delivered; a command, the execution of which was prevented by the sudden dispersion of his escort and capture of his person achieved by our cavalry at the battle of Ashta.

Holkar, a hopeless fugitive, was recalled, and established as Sovereign of a territory, really producing more from the beneficial administration introduced, than had ever before reached the coffers of the government. The districts of which he was nominally deprived, to form the independant territory of Ameer Khan, the feudatory allotment for Ghuffoor Khan, and a little addition to the Rajah of Kotah, had in fact been irrevocably alienated, and were held by those chieftains with a force, which would render any attempt of Holkar's government to dispossess them, idle. The Gwyckwar had not been involved in the conspiracy, and he profited as a friend, by our bestowal on him of some lands and rights, in the province of Guzerat, which had appertained to Bajee Rao. Appah Saheb, the expelled Rajah of Nagpore, is the only individual of the Mahratta Sovereigns remaining to be accounted for. When he stood in a perilous condition, from his proximity to the rule of that country, and the jealousy which the reigning Prince entertained of him, we secured his life by our avowed protection. The subsequent decline of that reigning Prince's intellect, into complete idiotcy, made it necessary for the British Government to use that privilege of interposition, to which we had entitled ourselves under a recent treaty. The Rajah was taken out of the hands of some low wretches, whom he had collected to amuse him, while he had yet a sense of volition; and who, under his name, were pillaging the treasures of the state: and the Rejency was placed in the hands of Appah Saheb. The Regent availing himself of the facility which his situation afforded, caused the Rajah to be poisoned, lest he should adopt a son, who might, notwithstanding the Rajah's incapacity of choice, find support from some party in the State. The crime was suspected; but, as there was not then any thing like proof of it, the surmise could not stand in the way of Appah Saheb's accession to the Musnud or Throne, so that he was immediately recognized by us as the lawful head of the government. Our further intercourse, was a succession of favors lavished by us, till the Peishwa resorted to arms. At that epoch, Appah Saheb, with the basest treachery, endeavoured to destroy the Resident, by an attack which he hoped would be unexpected. Being foiled in his attempt, and intimidated by the approach of large bodies of our troops, he opened a secret negociation with the Resident; offering to withdraw from his army, which he would order to separate into quarters; and to repose himself entirely upon the Resident, were he assured that his exercise of the sovereign power should remain undiminished. This proposal was accepted, on Appah Saheb's solemnly plighted faith, that he would not seek to aid the Peishwa, whom we were closely pressing in the field, or hold any communication with him. The army of the Rajah did not disperse; but on the contrary, stood an action under the walls of the capital; thereby affording ground for suspicion, that Appah Saheb had taken the double chance of resting upon us, should his forces be defeated, or of rejoining them, should they be victorious. Notwithstanding the doubt unavoidably entertained, the rout of the Rajah's troops made it appear our most desirable course, to confine him in his professed good dispositions, by seeming to give the fullest credit to his sincerity. While we were thus encouraging him, we obtained the most unquestionable proofs of his being in correspondence with the Peishwa; and of his having solicited that Prince to hasten with his army to Nagpore, where his Highness would be joined by the Nagpore forces, broken for the moment, but not extinguished. Pursuant to this invitation, the Peishwa marched in the direction of Nagpore; and was joined by a portion of the Rajah's troops, which happened to have retired in the vicinity of that line. As the machinations of the Rajah now became seriously dangerous, his arrest was indispensable. It took place, accordingly, when one of his principal Ministers, who was seized at the same time, openly reproached him for the folly and ingratitude of his conduct, whereby his Highness had involved both of them in such disgrace. He asked the Rajah whether he would deny his (the Minister's) having earnestly and repeatedly supplicated his Highness to abstain from the perfidious intrigues into which he was plunging himself. Appah Saheb admitted the truth of his Minister's assertion, saying, moreover, that he had been aware of the probable ruin attending on his procedure; but that his bond of obedience to his Chief, the Peishwa, was above all other considerations. Orders were issued for the Rajah's being sent to a fortress on the banks of the Ganges, where he was to be for the present detained, but with respectful treatment. The British officer commanding the escort was instructed not to subject the Rajah to restraint, which might be humiliating, without being absolutely necessary for preventing his escape. This desire on the part of Government was construed by the officer with such latitude, that he left to the Rajah the means of getting away. Appah Saheb betook himself to a hilly province of his country, where he collected a considerable body of mountaineers, and called on the inhabitants in general to rise in his favour. This made it expedient for us to lose no time in establishing a new Government. The members of the reigning family and the principal persons of the State were consulted. They unanimously recommended the nearest in blood in the Booshla (the Rajah's) family, for the succession; and he was raised to the Musnud in the room of Appah Saheb: we retaining the tract along the Nerbudda, which had fallen to us after the action at Jubbalpore, and which was necessary for the continuity of our territory. The country has since remained in quiet and prosperity, under this arrangement. Appah Saheb, forced from his strong holds, fled to Asseer Ghur, where he was secretly received by Jeswunt Rao Law, the Governor, who had long instigated his opposition to us. Not caring to abide the fate of the fortress when our troops advanced to besiege it, he quitted it in disguise, and made his way to Runjeet Sing, in Lahore. The latter could not, according to Indian habits, refuse him a shelter; but well understood that the granting this refuge to the Ex-Rajah could not be offensive to us, and would not need explanation if he, Runjeet Sing, prevented the Ex-Rajah from collecting any body of armed adherents. Appah Saheb has therefore remained in the territory of Runjeet Sing, subsisting on a slender allowance granted to him by that Chief, and strictly watched, though not declaredly a prisoner.

Thus the condition of the several Mahratta States has been pourtrayed. Each is hemmed round and effectually shackled, partly by the Honourable Company's possessions; partly by the Patan, or Rahjoot States, of considerable strength, and bound to us by the clearest community of interest. The peace of Central India seems well secured, while the extension of our paramountship to the Indies, has a bearing which shall be noticed hereafter.

When a crisis altogether inevitable had occurred, and unprovoked malignity had imposed upon us a struggle not for preponderance, but for the retention of any footing in India, the having risen superior to the danger, even at heavy cost, would be a rational ground for self-gratulation. In proportion as the effort had made a recurrence of similar hazard less probable, the charges suffered would be lightly regarded. Should a further advantage have been acquired; should a large addition to the annual revenue of the Honourable Company attend the removal of the peril which had impended, and the substantiation of an arrangement precluding as far as human calculations can go, all likelihood of a convulsion for many years, little might appear remaining to be wished; and the pecuniary sacrifice at which such a position was purchased, would not be very strictly considered. The satisfaction may admit an ingredient rendering it more complete. The bettered condition of several millions of the Natives, whence our supremacy has been spontaneously and joyfully acknowledged by the great bulk of the inhabitants, is a pride for the Honourable Company's reflection as well as a security for its interest. It is, I must confidently believe, so felt.

I proceed to shew, that in the attainment of points every way so important, the Honourable Company has not been put to the expense of a single shilling. Lest any doubt should be suggested on the comparative statements which I intended to submit, I required specific answers on certain heads from those public functionaries in India immediately charged with financial details. The letter in the Appendix, signed by the Secretary of the Government in the revenue department, and by the Accountant-General, is evidence equally precise and irrefragable. Each separate exposition which I offer will be verified by reference to that document. To be more generally understood, I convert their sums of rupees into English sterling. In doing this, the Sicca rupee is estimated at two shillings and sixpence; because, although that be not the rate at which it is at present receivable in England, it is better to take the computation according to which former accounts have been discussed in Parliament, than to look to a fluctuating exchange, while the assumed value of the coin is of no consequence in the comparison of sums at different periods, since the same rate is made applicable to each.

The financial year of India commences on the first of May—of course closes on the thirtieth of April. Having arrived at Calcutta late in 1813, I regard my financial management as having commenced on the first of May 1814; that is, with the beginning of the official year 1814-15. On that day, the registered Indian debt stood at 21,39,92,502 rupees, or £26,649,052. 15*s.*

On the 30th of April 1821, the registered debt stood at 25,85,06,549 rupees, or £32,313,318. 12*s.* 6*d.* There was consequently an augmentation of the public debt, amounting to £5,664,255. 17*s.* 6*d.*

This account is taken on the 30th of April 1821, at which date the increase of debt was at the highest; a subsequent operation of finance involving the possibility, that portions have been liquidated at home, by money remitted for the eventual purpose, rendering it impracticable to state the point with certainty at a later period. It is now to be seen what was on the same day to be set in the opposite scale to that increased burthen. The cash balance is the money remaining in the different treasuries of the three presidencies, after the demands of the official year are defrayed. The aggregate cash balance of the three presidencies, or the Indian cash balance, as it is called, amounted on the 30th of April 1814 to 4,80,67,149 rupees, that is, £6,008,393. 12*s.* 6*d.* On the 30th of April 1821, the Indian cash balance amounted to 9,78,62,227 rupees, or £12,232,778. 7*s.* 6*d.* This latter sum exceeds the sum on hand on the 30th of April 1814, by £6,224,384. 15*s.*

It appears by the above account, that on the 30th of April 1821, this addition of cash accumulated in the treasuries exceeded the registered debt by more than five hundred and sixty thousand pounds sterling; so that upon that day I could have wiped off the whole of the additional debt incurred during my administration; and have left the public coffers richer by above half a million than I found them. Though the rapid increase of our income might seem to recommend this measure, while there would have been a striking effect for myself, I could not reconcile my mind to a step which I conceived essentially objectionable. The augmented value of the Government securities in the market, could not affect us as far as respected loss, since we had it at our option to discharge the bonds at par. But I deemed it highly impolitic (and I remain firm in the opinion) to break a tie which so obviously secures the attachment of the monied class to our Government, in a country where that class has peculiar influence. Latterly I have had reason to believe, that the Native Princes have fallen into the habit of vesting their money in those securities; a motive the more for them to abstain from intrigues against us. The periodical discharge of the interest can never be an embarrassment to the Company: nor is the magnitude of the debt objectionable in any other respect, when the high premium which these bonds command distinctly proves the number afloat scarcely suffices for the convenience of our native subjects. When I left India, the premium on those bonds, the interest of which was payable in Calcutta alone, fluctuated between fourteen and sixteen per cent; a material difference from the regular discount of twelve per cent. at which I found them. Although the accommodation of our native subjects, in such a depository for their money, and the facilitation to commercial transactions advantageous to the Honourable Company which such a convenience affords, be but a secondary consideration, it strengthens the argument for identifying the interest of a leading body of the natives with ours, by making such a proportion of their fortunes depend on our stability; and I anxiously hope that these circumstances will be fully weighed before any part of the accumulation shall be worse than wasted by applying it according to theoretic rules totally unsuitable to the present state of our Indian affairs. The fact of such an accumulation during a period of uncommon exertion must appear singular. The solution which might the most readily present itself would be, that the Government in India had, throughout the time in question, at least narrowed, if not wholly withheld the usual supplies to England. How that article stands has not been left to conjecture: for the twenty years preceding that which commenced on the 1st of May 1813, the average annual supplies from India to England (beyond those from England to India), amounted to 38,83,465 rupees, or £485,433 2*s.* 6*d.*

The average annual supply (similarly measured) from India to England, during the eight years; from the 30th of April 1814, to the 30th of April, 1822, was 1,05,90,515 rupees, or, £1,323,814. 7*s.* 6*d.*

Had the comparison been drawn, from what India contributed to England, during the first five years, after the 30th of April 1814, (the years within which, all the active operations were comprized), the result would have been prodigiously more marked in favour of the Local Government. It was, however, desirable, to bring down the account to the latest day on which it could be made out; and thence, a very extraordinary and unexpected charge came to be included in the description of supplies to India. This shall presently be explained. It is first, however, expedient to notice why the year 1813-14, is not taken as one of the twenty, preceding my administration, lest it should be thought there was some advantage in leaving it out. The year could not with any accuracy of definition be numbered as preceding my administration, since during the half of it I conducted public affairs. I was not entitled to assume for myself any merit for management in the earlier months; and in my portion of it, I remitted to the Honourable Court, a large sum in gold (I think about three hundred thousand pounds) beyond the ordinary supplies; which sum is not admitted into the credit of my statement, and could not, of course, be correctly set against me. Thence the year was necessarily a neutral one, as regarded the calculation. The secret of the accumulation is this: Though the military operations were of immense scale, there was great attention not to incur the charge of preparations, other than what were foreseen to be indispensable, and constant vigilance was exercised to prevent slatternly expenditure. From that care, the yearly income was sufficient to answer the additional demand of the war, and the produce of the loan remained in the treasury. The provision of cash from that resource had been so strongly urged, as a measure of salutary precaution, by those most experienced in the pecuniary details of the government, that I had, through deference, though not without some doubt of the necessity, assented. But when a loan was invited, by the Council at Calcutta, while I was at Cawnpore, it appeared to me so decidedly superfluous, that I requested the books might be closed as soon as possible. Luckily, the accumulation of the sum has not entailed any inconvenience; and the money is available for purposes of the highest importance.

The occurrence to which I alluded, as having affected, in appearance, the balance of supplies between England and India, was this. It was an article in the engagement, that the bond-holder should have the option of receiving the interest in India, or from the Honourable Court in London, as might suit his convenience. That choice had been given to accommodate the British lender, it never having entered into conception that the native bond-holder could resort to it. In the year 1819-20, however, the course of exchange became heavily disadvantageous for Calcutta. The Europeans residing in the city immediately perceived the means of profiting by the circumstance. By giving the native bond-holder something more than would have been receivable at the treasury, they obtained from the former, bills on the Honourable Court in London for the amount of the interest due. This practice was carried to the extent of the whole debt, occasioning a loss of nearly 22 per cent. to the Honourable Company, beside the inconvenience of having such a mass of bills to meet. The abuse demanded instant remedy. When it has been shewn how low was the credit of Government, in 1813-14, our command of the money market, in 1819-20, may be viewed with some surprise. It was so complete, that Government was enabled to notify bonds, to the amount of fifteen millions sterling, for immediate liquidation, unless the holders would exchange them for new bonds, the interest of which should be demandable in Calcutta alone. The new bonds were universally accepted by persons on the spot; an adequate term was allotted to agents, to take the pleasure of their principals at home, as to being paid off, or ceding their title to receive the interest in England. And it is this which prevented the state of the debt from being particularized later than the 30th of April, 1821. It is obvious, that it might be lower on a subsequent day, but could not in the interval have received addition. Bonds of a date posterior to those notified as above could not be dealt with exactly in the same manner, for Government feared to produce distress, by diminishing too much the means of remittance. To the holders of those bonds, the choice was given of receiving payment, or of accepting new bonds entitling the holder to exercise the option of demanding the interest at the Calcutta treasury, or of drawing on the Honourable Court for the amount, at the exchange of 2*s.* 1*d.* per the sicca rupee, instead of 2*s.* 6*d.* The new bonds were almost generally taken; and I left them bearing a premium of eighteen to twenty per cent. The annual loss against which the Honourable Company has been protected by this operation, for as long as a rate of exchange similar to the present may last, has been calculated at two hundred and fifty thousand pounds. Till the remedy was applied, the amount of interest drawn on the Honourable Court, and paid at home, was charged against

India as a supply from England, so as to diminish, in that proportion, the excess of supplies from India. As a particular in the improved condition of affairs in India, I mentioned the augmentation which the Honourable Company's revenue has received. The addition is not inconsiderable. The joint receipt of the three presidencies, for the official year 1813-14, excluding items which did not arise from Indian sources of revenue, amounted to 14,74,07,322 rupees, or £18,425,915. *5s.* 0*d.*

The receipt of 1821-22, restricted in the same manner, was 18,88,09,832 rupees, or £23,601,229; the income of the latter year consequently surpassed that of the year 1813-14 by £5,175,313.

Had it not been for a peculiar oversight, the excess would have been much greater. To prevent interference with the Honourable Company's trade in opium, we had made a treaty with the several independent chiefs in Western Hindostan, to purchase at a settled price the drug from them, to the fullest extent in which they had respectively hitherto produced it; prohibiting the admission of any quantity beyond that amount into our territories. As the possessions of the chiefs in question were contiguous to the Bombay presidency, that government was requested to manage the sale for the export of opium so acquired. From being unaccustomed to the arrangement, the Bombay government made its terms that the whole price for the opium of 1821-22 sold by it should be payable in May 1822, thereby excluding that article of income from the official year to which it justly belonged. As the amount was 38 lacks of rupees, or four hundred and seventy-five thousand pounds sterling, the difference occasioned by its omission from the account of its proper year is not trifling. I have no hesitation in saying that the income of the current year 1822-23 may be anticipated as exceeding by six millions sterling that of 1813-14. This increase ought to be still further progressive, because, while none of the sources at present productive are likely to become less so, but on the contrary exhibit every promise of yielding more, there is a reduction which must in its nature be annually diminishing in operation, till at length it shall wholly cease. In the territory of Poonah, for instance, in order to secure acquiescence in the extraordinary change which we were effecting, life terms in land were either confirmed or granted to men of influence to the extent of fifty-one lacks, or £637,500 annually. These are interceptions from the receipt, and it is to be observed that all the comparisons submitted by me refer not to calculable income, but to actual receipt. Life rents of this kind must successively (many of them speedily) fall in, and swell the sum paid into the Honourable Company's coffers. Tenures of the same description, though not so numerous, had been granted when Lord Lake subdued the territories around Delhi; and such of them as are still outstanding are subject to similar lapse. Were this increase of receipts accompanied by an exactly corresponding increase of charges, still it would not cease to be an advantage to Britain. It would not be a direct gain for the Honourable Company, though much profit would, through circuitous channels, reach the coffers of that body. I should thence have been little satisfied, had I not been able to provide for the safe and undisturbed retention of our newly acquired territories, on terms which would ensure to the Honourable Company a constant and ample surplus. After revolving every circumstance with the coolest caution, I cannot find any reason why, subsequently to the present year, an annual surplus of four millions sterling should not be confidently reckoned upon. This ought naturally to encrease, for the causes which will augment the receipt have nothing in them tending to require further charges.

Whatsoever melioration the affairs of the Honourable Company may have experienced, such efforts of mine as contributed to it were no more than simply my duty. The tenor of my engagement implied, in my construction, my plighted honour to use my unremitting exertions for the advantage of those who placed their reliance on me; and the critical nature of any unforeseen objects towards which those exertions could become demanded, be the risk of my decision what it might, was of course within our mutual understanding. I have therefore no merit to claim, beyond consciousness of having indefatigably endeavoured to fulfil that to which I felt myself pledged. At the same time I may be permitted to avow my exultation, at having been able to conciliate with the strictest discharge of my trust the bettered condition of an immense population: a circumstance in which I regard the character and interest of our country to have gained much. I believe it to be an honest boast to have been even such an humble instrument as I was in the effectuation of that end.

Still the vanity of contributing towards so proud a purpose might seduce me to pay less attention than was due to my more immediate obligation. Thence I will beg leave to recapitulate the points of benefit for the Honourable Company which I consider established; that, if I have been any where deficient, the particular neglect may at once be seized:—

1st. The overweening insolence and hostility of Nepaul, a power dangerous, from its position along an extensive and open frontier of ours, has been so completely chastened, as to make that people sensible they can only retain their independence as a state through the moderation of the British Government.

2d. The Pindarry Association, a dreadful scourge to every neighbouring community, and peculiarly afflictive to the Hon. Company's subjects, has been annihilated; and the fruitless annual expense of protective measures against those depredators, together with frequent heavy loss of revenue, is henceforth precluded.

3d. A confederacy, aiming at no less than the total extirpation of the British from India, has been so thoroughly subverted, that not a germ is left for its reproduction.

4th. Throughout the term of an administration during which such unprecedented demands for services on the spot were to be met, the Hon. Court has received, on an average, annual supplies from India (beyond the amount of supplies from England to India) nearly trebling the rate of supplies furnished to it on the average of twenty years preceding. For five years of my administration, which most demanded extraordinary effort in India, the supplies nearly quintupled the former example.

5th. The yearly Indian revenue of the Hon. Company, from permanent sources, exhibited at the close of the last official year an increase of five millions one hundred and seventy-five thousand pounds sterling by actual receipt. For reasons assigned, that increase is expected to amount in the present year, 1822-23, to six millions. There is no probability that it should hereafter sink below that rate; but there is every just ground to reckon upon its progressive augmentation.

6th. The clear Indian surplus to be henceforth exhibited is estimated by me at four millions sterling yearly. It will probably be more ample.

7th. The Hon. Court has been, with a material saving, delivered from an embarrassing perversion of the conditions of former loans; while the justice of the operation was so distinctly recognized that the credit of the Hon. Company's Indian Securities has risen to a pitch which no speculation could ever have presumed.

8th. In the year 1813-14, the independent powers of India were so numerous and strong, as to conceive themselves equal to expel the British. At present, every native state in that vast region is in either acknowledged or essential subjugation to our Government.

Lastly. These advantages are not counterbalanced by any burthens contracted in the acquiring them; because there is at this instant an accumulation of cash in the treasuries beyond what I set out with, more than sufficient to wipe off the additional debt incurred during my administration, were it wise so to employ the money.

The credit sought for this flourishing condition of the finances might be fallacious. The exposition is delusive and unworthy, if the plenitude of the coffers be owing to the produce of novel and grinding taxes, or to Government's having kept back from the country those issues of money which every community is entitled to expect shall be applied by its rulers in furtherance of public convenience. As to the first, it suffices to say, that not a single new impost took place during my administration, while several teasing demands were abolished, as well in the old provinces as in the acquired territories. Regarding the second, I have reason to hope that I cannot be charged with having neglected those facilitations to commercial intercourse, and those encouragements to agricultural activity, which I knew would be consonant to the just and liberal spirit of the Hon. Company. Readiness of communication is in every country the chief spur to industry. Roads, of which many approach to completion, are in progress, under the superintendence of the Quarter-Master-General's department; and as I do not recollect any of the branches to be of much less extent than two hundred miles, with numerous bridges, over streams heretofore often impassable for long terms, through the casual swelling of the waters, the degree of accommodation to be thus afforded to the inhabitants would be thought important in any part of the world. It is peculiarly so in Central India, where the prevalence of clayey soil makes the tracks which the natives denominate roads, frequently impracticable for even their light carriages during the rainy season. The transportation of goods has been further promoted by attention to canals; though in the latter an utility has been consulted far beyond the dispatch of articles to a distant market. The canal of Ali Murdhun, after being devoid of water, and its banks every where prostrated, for above threescore years, has been perfectly restored. The city of Delhi, though situated on the banks of the Jumna, was destitute of wholesome water. The river, in those alterations common to all the greater streams in their course through the wide plain of Northern India, had come into contact with such vast beds of natron, that its water became powerfully impregnated with the salt, and consequently nauseous. To remedy the distress, Ali Murdhun conceived the grand design of forming a canal which should receive a large portion of the stream of the Jumna, where it issues pure from the mountains into the plain, and should convey it to the Moghul capital. This was achieved. The extensive tract through which it passed had been chiefly untilled, because in most parts the wells sunk in it furnished only water so saturated with natron as to be unfit to drink, and adverse to vegetation. The facility of irrigating the land with the water of the canal soon collected settlers and produced cultivation: so that a large expanse, till then desert, displayed the most luxuriant fertility. The gratitude of the inhabitants bestowed on the canal the expressive title of "Sea of Plenty." The feelings of the people of Delhi, on the restoration of this canal, may be judged from the fact, that on the day fixed for removing the last intercepting mound, and suffering the water to proceed to the city, the whole of them went forth to hail the boon, by throwing garlands and sweetmeats into the advancing current. A long branch from this most useful work had formerly, under the name of Ferooze Sha's canal, been pushed into the province of Hurracana. Its supply was lost in the destruction of the magnificent source whence it had been fed; and its course remained but partially traceable. At the time of my departure from India this canal was nearly re-established, every mile of its progress being attended with revived teeming cultivation, in a region which had been abandoned. A third canal, which runs longitudinally through the Doab, and had been constructed in ancient times to accommodate a country where streams were scarce, was also in process of restoration when I sailed. Calcutta was naturally not overlooked by me. The causes of the insalubrity of that city had been carefully investigated and ascertained. Contagious disorders were unavoidably generated by the excessive closeness with which the hovels of the natives were huddled together in the heart of the city, and the numerous small pools of stagnant water concealed among those hovels. Large sums having been advanced to the Committee of Improvement, a well considered plan was adopted for correcting both the unhealthiness and the inconveniences. The main remedy lay in piercing Calcutta through the centre, in its longest diameter, with a street sixty feet wide. The ventilation of the city, as well as the comfort of the inhabitants, was still further promoted by making several squares with a tank or spacious reservoir of water in the middle of each; to be surrounded by planted walks for the recreation of the better classes. These improvements, however, still as to ornament and convenience, fell short in comparison with the Quay, called the Strand, destined to extend upon the river bank along the city between two and three miles. Much of it is already finished to a height of about forty feet above low-water-mark, with many ghauts, or broad flights of stairs, for the accommodation of the Natives in the bathing prescribed by their religion, as well as for the landing of goods. Being sixty feet clear at the top, this Quay will afford great facilitation for the carriage of articles from the shipping to all parts of the city. There is another work which, though not actually begun, is fitting to be noticed here. Dangerous shoals, between the mouth of the Hooghly and Calcutta, prevent all ships of considerable size from coming up to the city; and merchant vessels of but moderate bulk are exposed to no little risk in the attempt. At the same time the violent squalls, and the bore to which the Hooghly is liable, render the dispatch of cargoes back and forward, by the river sloops, tardy and hazardous. As a remedy for this difficulty, it has been proposed to form, from Calcutta to New Anchorage, where the great ships ordinarily moor, a canal competent to be navigated by those sloops. A survey having been made by my direction, the plan appeared securely and speedily feasible, partly by cuts—partly by availing ourselves of favourable reaches in different small rivers. The length would be about ninety miles. As the tolls would furnish a large interest for the money expended, I left upon record my opinion that the undertaking should be earnestly recommended to the Honourable Court of Directors.

Conviction may be felt, from this statement, that the fostering attention which the Honourable Company would desire should be paid to the immense population over which it presides, has not been sacrificed to selfish interests. I do not particularize the dissemination of instruction among the natives, because any impulse which I could lend to its promotion, was nothing in measurement by the standard of those most meritorious and consecutive endeavours of others whence visible and increasing impression has been widely made in the country. The point is mentioned only lest I should leave myself open to the suspicion of not having adverted to a duty of such deep concern.

I have ventured to suppose the interests of our country at large as having been promoted by the recent settlement in India. In no way could I gratify the Honourable Company more than in shewing that it did not seek the enjoyment of an exclusive benefit; but prided itself on reaping its advantages under the influence of our national prosperity. It is strictly accurate to contemplate the case with this extended view. The concerns of the Honourable Company have, I trust, been solidly improved; but it has only been through arrangements which add directly to the power of Britain. I am prompted not to let slip the opportunity of making the assertion, from my being aware that, except in a confined circle, the affairs of India are insufficiently understood in England. The worth of so splendid an appendage to the British crown is not adequately estimated. Strange as it may seem, I myself remember to have heard the argument vehemently supported a few years ago, that India was an injurious drain to the mother country. It is difficult to figure to one's self how so loose a notion had been adopted. Were one to rest on advantages of an inferior description alone, our footing in India affords several to England, unbalanced, as far as I can judge, by any inconvenience. An honourable and dignified maintenance is provided for branches of many respectable families; thereby removing a burthen from the patrimonial estate, with a prospect of ultimate wealth to uphold the name. Then let advertence be given to the fact, that almost every one of those functionaries renders assistance to some connexion or other at home. The remittances from this liberality, which is fully within my knowledge, may seem of little consequence: yet the aggregate of a number of streamlets constant in their course cannot be indifferent; especially if the supply from these unobserved channels have an obvious tendency to aid that rapid circulation which is the secret of general opulence in every country. But the magnitude of establishments in India, and that of the military force above the rest, has been censured. Perhaps it might be worthy of reflection, that in proportion to the extent of those establishments will be the scale of those unceasing silent contributions which I have described; while it is not to be forgotten, that this is not the return of English money to England. Whatsoever be the expense of the Indian establishments, the funds for them are all furnished from Indian sources. The supplies from England to India, mentioned in a former part of this detail, are only advances made by the Honourable Court, chiefly in stores and other articles of consumption, which are repaid by India. An argument founded on this consideration would not be valid, if urged against any sound objection to the expense of the establishments as wasteful or abusive. I know not on what ground the charges could justly be so represented. The numerical strength of civil servants has been regarded by every one who has considered the subject, as far short of what the service demands. The scale of the military force has not been hastily or carelessly determined. It is not in India merely necessary to measure the degree of force requisite to guard against the possible ebullitions of a population, and generally an armed population, which I believe to equal that of all Europe. It is indispensable to have stations throughout that wide expanse, which may assist the native princes in the control of their own soldiery, and thus enable them to fulfil their engagements, of keeping the roads in their respective dominions free from robbers: a burthen for which we are amply compensated by the activity and security of a trade productive to us in a variety of ways. The main consideration, however, still remains to be explained. There is in India a numerous class, by descent, and by habit from early youth, professedly devoted to a military life. Individuals of this body rarely, and in small numbers, find means of subsistence in other situations, such as, according to the prejudices of the country, they can fill without disgrace. It is policy, nay more, it is economy, to leave an adequate opening for the employment of such a proportion of the men in question, as that the residue which cannot be taken into pay may not be able to form any where commotions requiring exertion and expenditure for their dissipation. The particulars which must determine the desirable extent of force are so complicated and fluctuating, that the point should visibly be left to the prudence of the local Government. When the Honourable Court pressed military reduction upon me, I could only say, that, with an ample force, I would ensure to the Honourable Company a revenue yielding a large surplus. Should the force be rendered incompetent, I could not answer for satisfactory results in any shape. My notion of the proper scale may be erroneous, but the issue has not been unfavourable.

No one can be blind to the circumstance, that the magnitude of a force wholly supplied with arms, clothing, and equipments by the British manufacturer, involves somewhat of an intelligible set-off against the abstract objection of its burthen on the Indian finances. The quality of that objection, however, is not precisely comprehensible. If it be said, that, on the present footing, the large provision for the army intercepts sums which might otherwise augment the dividends, I should conceive that the proprietors would not be much disposed to risk their actual advantages upon the hazardous experiment of diminishing the force by which advantages of such extraordinary present amount are now secured; and the individuals interested are the most likely to form a salutary judgment on their own concerns. Should it be said, that by the expenditure the Honourable Company is insomuch the less able to discharge the territorial bonds due to the English creditor, the reasoning would in the first place gratuitously and improbably assume, that, with a scanty force, an equal accumulation of surplus would be forthcoming to answer the debt. But I appeal to the proof already given, that every one of those creditors who wished for the liquidation of the bonds possessed by him, might have had them discharged immediately. The case, indeed, is hardly imaginable, that an individual could desire payment at par from the Company, when, by exchanging his old bond for a new one, he could on the same day sell his security at a great premium. Thence, the instances in which the new bonds were not accepted, have been simply those where time was allowed for reference to a creditor in Europe, who had not left with any agent powers applicable to such a contingency. Every bond that was purchased ten years ago in the market, and was transferred as above, became, and remains worth a fourth more than was paid for it when so bought. This part of the subject cannot be dismissed without observing, that it is idle to regard as embarrassing, a debt which scarcely exceeds one year's income of the State; the interest of which, consequently, bears so small a proportion to that income, as to render the provision for it a matter of no possible inconvenience. The invariable condition of the loans leaves discharge of capital entirely dependent on the will of the Honourable Company, so long as the interest shall be punctually paid at the fixed periods.

I have been solicitous to shew that there was not any thing questionable in the stability or affluence of the Honourable Company's finances, because an unsoundness in that respect would detract from the value which I ascribe to India as a portion of the British empire. No such doubt being rationally admissible, every Statesman must surely perceive how many of the European Sovereigns are held seriously in check by the powerful armies which it is now known India could rapidly dispatch against their possessions. The situation, if it be duly considered, makes the command of so large a disposable force no inconsiderable ingredient in our national strength. From the relaxation of prejudices among the Sepoys, that force is not to be deemed available for contiguous objects alone; but is transportable by sea to distant parts of hostile dominions. Should it be imagined that while India contains those means of offensive operation, it may on the other hand be exposed to insurrections or invasion, which would forbid the embarkation of those troops for prolonged enterprize, I answer that experience in times far less tranquil than the present, repels such an assumption. Remembrance that an Indian army actually exhibited itself in Egypt, must satisfy every one how readily applicable that force is to remote purposes. Were it even granted that the sending those troops up the Red Sea was done at some risk to the territories whence the army was drawn, I would say, whatsoever might have been the case then, no danger is conceivable now. As to internal commotion, its nature could not be apprehended as passing, at the utmost, some unconnected attempts at assemblages for the purpose of plunder; an evil which would be provided against by the enrolment of irregular levies, for the time during which the disciplined force should be absent. As to attack from abroad, the intention must be long previously discovered, so that India could not be found unprepared. The project would be futile, did it not embrace the calculation of disposition and ability in the inhabitants of India to facilitate the undertaking. Such an expectation would, in the existing position of affairs, be groundless. Had any native Prince the wish to abet a foreign assailant of our territory, his indulgence of the propensity would be utterly insignificant. There is not a Chief liable to the suspicion of doubtful inclination, who is not surrounded by warlike States bound in the strictest compact to us. The nullity of formal conditions, when opposed to strong impulses of frowardness or temptation, is not overlooked by me. But the Feudatory States have become so through their own solicitation, on terms principally offered by themselves, and from speculations of benefit, which our Government has been active in realizing to them. There is nothing humiliating in the relation, since a paramount power in India has been for centuries a notion so familiar, that the existence of such an authority appears to the natives almost indispensable. This confederation of the Feudatory States extends in an unbroken chain quite to the Indus. There is not, in the vicinity of that river's left bank, any tribe from which an invader could look to encouragement; on the contrary, the attempt of any secondary column to pass that river where its stream is united, and thereby to distract attention from the main body, which would hold a more northerly course, could not fail to experience serious and persevering obstruction from an energetic people. I repeat, that I am not relying on the articles of the treaty: my confidence is in a clearly understood identity of permanent interest, for which no foreign power could hold forth an equivalent. There is, however, in India, a principle capable of superseding the most thorough conviction of interest, or even the strongest personal wishes: certain acknowledged public obligations are held by the Native Princes so binding on what they call their Hoormut, or plighted honour to society, that no consideration can induce them to palter with the constructive pledge. Among these were the professed, though antiquated dependencies on the house of Timour: the sovereign of Oude was the nominal Vizier of the Moghul Empire. It must be obvious, that should any European potentate aim at the subversion of the British establishment in India, it would not be with so absurdly extravagant a hope, as the succeeding to a similar domination. To reduce Britain's strength by depriving her of such sinews as India affords, would be the purpose; and the course which would suggest itself for effecting it, would be the exciting some powerful sentiment in India against us. Perhaps the only pretence which any forecasting enemy can have imagined likely to awaken sensation, would be the restoration of efficient rule to the house of Timour. While such a war-cry would have been a call on the fealty of the sovereign of Oude, as professedly Vizier of the empire, the claim upon him would have had the additional force of an ostensibly Mahommedan cause. To break ties which might eventually be so injurious to us, appeared to me of the highest importance. Though Oude had not any army, since our subsidiary force supplies the place of one for the defence and interior regulation of the country, that territory required careful attention in a military view. The country contains at least six millions of inhabitants, every adult male of whom is provided with arms, and habituated to the use of them. The force, however irregular, capable to be thence collected in the rear of the army with which we were meeting the invader on the frontier, was a subject not to be revolved without anxiety. The knowledge of an insurrection behind them, to an extent which could not be ascertained, as our communication with the Lower Provinces would be precarious and interrupted, if not wholly cut off, would unavoidably agitate the minds, and diminish the confidence of the advanced troops. I had often ruminated on that chance. I thence eagerly availed myself of a mortification, which I could perceive the Nawab Vizier felt acutely, from its having occurred within my sight. Two brothers of the King of Delhi resided at Lucknow, supported by allowances granted partly by the Honourable Company, partly by the Nawab Vizier: notwithstanding their partial dependance on the latter for subsistence, etiquette assigned to these princes a decided pre-eminence, insomuch, that when the Nawab Vizier met them in the street, it was incumbent that the elephant on which he was riding should be made to kneel, in token of homage. It was to an occasion of this sort that I have just alluded; I caught at the opportunity of saying to the Nawab Vizier, that to continue such demonstration of inferiority must rest with himself alone, for the British Government did not require the manifestation of such submission to the Delhi family, and had itself dropped those servile forms with which it had heretofore unbecomingly complied. Having reason to think that this instigation would work upon the Nawab Vizier's reflection, I directed the Resident to watch and encourage any apparent disposition in that prince to emancipate himself. The mode which would naturally suggest itself to the Nawab Vizier, as being the only one sufficient to account satisfactorily to India at large for his rejection of future prostration to the house of Timour, was his assumption of the kingly title. It was likely that he would distantly sound the Resident on the subject: I therefore instructed the latter, that were any supposition of the sort hypothetically thrown out, he should seize it and bring it immediately to a distinct understanding; intimating his persuasion that the British Government would readily recognise such a title, if assumed by the sovereign of Oude, provided it made no change in the relations and formularies between the two States, or altered the manner in which British subjects, permitted by our Government to visit Lucknow, had hitherto been received. The expected procedure soon took place; the Sovereign of Oude's assumption to the title of King was treated by the court of Delhi with undisguised indignation. The offensive animadversions were keenly resented by the Court of Lucknow, and an irreparable breach between those two Mahommedan States is avowed. Had it not been for this public separation, and the renunciation of all connection, the Sovereign of Oude might in some day have found himself, contrary to his most earnest wish, involved in warfare against us by the general sense of his nobles, as well as by the prejudices of his people. While the hostility of the country would have had the inconvenience which I have already described, the character of the Sovereign, admirable for uprightness, humanity, and mild elevation, would have bestowed colour on the adverse cause, and his treasures might have been efficaciously employed in the payment of troops assembled against us in other quarters.

To have contributed towards parrying this contingency afforded me considerable satisfaction. For, at that period, there had not been sufficient lapse of time to prove that the new arrangements in Central India were so perfectly fixed as to make all contemplation of extraneous hostility indifferent.

There is not now any inconvenience in exposing these details. Our internal domination is firm, from its standing on the surest of all bases, the conviction prevalent among the natives (with exceptions so few, as not to weigh against the meaning of the general assertion), that their own comforts are inseparably interwoven with it. In the profession of this sentiment, no Sovereign is more strenuous than the King of Oude. His sagacity would immediately have discovered, in our encouragement of the line he was disposed to take, any selfish design of misleading him into the sacrifice of his own solid interests, for our advantage, and he would have quietly defeated the project. On the contrary, he felt that relations with the house of Timour must be as delusive with regard to eventual support, as they were humiliating in their immediate accompaniments: and he justly comprehended, that he best consulted his dignity, as well as his direct gratification, by declaring his kingdom, as he has done in a letter to our Sovereign, to be a spontaneously attached dependency on the British empire. This leaning to intimate union with us, has been produced in the minds of the Native Princes by a plain and natural policy on our part. Heretofore, we had been too prone to assume an air of superiority revolting to them. It was not the disposition of our functionaries in the Mofussil, as the parts beyond the city of Calcutta are termed; for, in numerous instances, the urbanity of the individuals counteracted the mischief of an erroneous system. A conception had been entertained by our Government, that reserved manner, and a tone of dictation, would impress the natives with a wholesome notion of our power, and would bend them to unquestioning acquiescence in our will. There was further a confused opinion, that what is regarded in Europe as the Law of Nations, was not pleadable by States in amity with us; still less by those in alliance, where considerations of ours suggested authoritative interposition, provided the interposition observed essential justice; a qualification very liable to mistake, when the essential justice was to be determined only by our view of the particular case. Undoubtedly, measures must be squared according to junctures, and to the habits of the society on which they are intended to operate; and it would be an unfair conclusion, that the facilities which presented themselves to me, for the trial of a different principle, existed at the dates to which I refer: whatever were the causes of failure, the expectation of extensive influence over the natives had been disappointed. They had been subdued, but not conciliated. It was, therefore, desirable to see what might be done, by abstaining from any conduct which would unnecessarily wound the pride of a chief, or disgust his followers. To extinguish the jealousy of the chief, by paying public respect to his station, and upholding his authority, was to secure not his attachment alone, but that of his subjects, who felt their own pride trampled upon in his degradation. I therefore pointedly enjoined the strictest observance of polite and unassuming demeanor on the part of our functionaries towards the rulers, with courtesy to the better classes of the people, and kindness of manner to the lower. Still more particularly, I directed that, unless where a special provision in a treaty had secured to us a right of intervention, no interference should be attempted with the ordinary course of Government in any State. That there should be even an affectation of avoiding to notice what was going forward in the interior administration of affairs; it being sure, that in cases of embarrassment, the native rulers would apply to the British functionary, when he could do so, without incurring in the eyes of his people the appearance of subjection. The expedience of that inculcation, as well as the generous alacrity with which it was obeyed, is evinced by the singularly rapid subsidence of all Central India into complete tranquillity, after a convulsion, which had terminated in such unprecedented alterations. I had, indeed, to reckon on the most energetic assistance, in my views, from both the Civil and Military servants of the Honourable Company; because my plans were in exact consonance to their inclinations: such a tone towards the natives, was what the heart of each of them would have warmly prompted. I could not forgive myself, were I to let slip such an opportunity of rendering to the Honourable Company's servants that testimony, which they had proudly merited from me. No body of men, taken generally, can be more high-minded, more conscientiously zealous, more just, more liberal, or more rigidly intolerant of any turpitude among their fellows. With these fundamental good qualities, they naturally feel pleasure in indulging a benign and conciliatory address towards the natives. I had but to sanction the propensity, by declaring, that Government comprehended its wisdom, not less than its humanity. The effect from these measures has been of late so visible throughout the country, that no man will be found to doubt it, or to hesitate in saying whence it arises. Reckoning thus, that it is the equity and amenity experienced from us, by the natives, which so sways their adherence, I cannot be wrong in representing the circumstance as creditable to British reputation. And the internal tranquillity, for the permanence of which such a style of intercourse is a satisfactory pledge, insures to our country so unreserved a command over the resources of India, as will justify the statement, that augmented advantage to Britain has resulted from the recent transactions. The simple principle upon which I acted, continued in full efficacy when I quitted India; and I cannot apprehend that, after such proofs of its beneficial consequences, it will ever be abandoned.

As to myself, I can readily imagine that I may not have adequately improved openings, which fortune presented; that I may not have achieved all the salutary purposes, which the devoted gallantry of the troops at my disposal could have enabled me to secure; that I may not have attained ends, profitable for the Honourable Company, with as little hazard or expenditure as would have attended their acquirement in hands more skilful. But it is not a claim of ability that I am maintaining; my engagement was to defend and promote, to the best of my capacity, the concerns with which I was entrusted. I have sought to shew, that, in a crisis of unparalleled complication, extent and difficulty, the exertion in which the fulfilment of my obligation consisted, was not forborne. The issue will bear out my pretension. For the settlement of such a violently disturbed mass will never be referred to chance, but will be attributed to the efforts, which, however they might be deficient in judiciousness, must have been anxiously pondered, consistent, and indefatigable.

APPENDIX.

APPENDIX.

APPENDIX.

(A.)

SKETCH of the Extra Expenses occasioned by Hostile Preparations, and the Prosecution of Offensive Operations, during the last four official years, *i.e.* from the year 1814-1815 to the year 1817-1818, appertaining exclusively to the Presidency of Bengal, *viz.*

For 1814-1815.

War against Nepaul first Campaign, including the Offensive Position of Major-General Marshall's Division :

The aggregate amount of war charges in the year 1814-1815, including Commissariat Disbursements, and other incidental expences was .... S.R. 30,93,381 9 3

The above aggregate embraces also the disbursements, on account of the following corps, subsequently disbanded, *viz.*

Lieutenant-Colonel W. L. Gardiner's Levies, consisting of Rohillah's and Alli Gholes Levies, raised under the Orders of the Hon. E. Gardiner.

Corps of Najabs and Mahwattis, raised by Mr. Hearsay.

Corps embodied under the Orders of Major-General Sir David Ochterlony.—Part only of these were disbanded, the remainder were retained as the foundation of the 4th Hill Corps.

Troops raised by Mirza Alli Beg. A corps of Najubs under Amur Khan. Irregular Horse and Burkundanzes raised by the Rajah Gunsum Sing.

Troops raised by Shaik Kullah Alli Khan.

Two russelahs of cavalry raised by the Resident at Lucknow.

For 1815-1816.

Second Campaign against Nepaul.

Amount of War charges, including Commissariat extraordinaries, and other incidental charges.................. S.R. 20,63,580 10 11

The above aggregate embraces also the expence incurred on account of the following corps subsequently disbanded :

Irregular russalahs and Dakree goorlahs under Major-General Sir David Ochterlony.

A russalah of irregular cavalry under Bunker Alli Khan.

Horse raised by Dalial Alli and Kusureen Khan, Zemindars in the district of Shahabad.

Horse raised by Mr. Brooke, at Benares.

Horse raised by Mr. Moorcroft, at Poosah.

For 1816-1817.

Siege of Hattrass.

Amount of War charges, including Commissariat extraordinaries, and other incidental expences..................S.R. 3,18,915 12 10

For 1817-1818.

Offensive Operations against the Pindarries and Mahratta Chieftains.

Amount of War charges, including Commissariat extraordinaries, and every incidental expence ..............S.R. 34,34,874 0 9

(Signed) H. IMLACK,
Military Auditor General.

(A true copy) HASTINGS.

(B.)

EXTRACT from the Report made by Major-General Sir David Ochterlony, of the Tour which he had been directed to make through the Feudatory States in Meywar and Malwa.

" I have only to add, that throughout my tour I have derived the most sincere gratification, from observing the prevalent tranquillity and increasing prosperity of the country. From the prince to the peasant, I have found every tongue eloquent in the expression of gratitude to the British Government for the blessings they enjoy. Discontent or oppression appear equally unknown, except at Oojein, and a few other places in the immediate occupancy of Scindiah's relatives.

(A true Copy.) HASTINGS.

(C.)

Calcutta, 26th November, 1822.

My Lord:

In reply to your Lordship's letter of the 23d instant, we have the honour to submit the following statements:—

1st. The joint receipt of the three Presidencies for the official year 1813-1814, excluding items which did not arise out of Indian sources of revenue, amounting to Rupees 14,74,07,322.

2nd. The Receipt of 1821-22, restricted in the same manner, was rupees 18,88,09,832.

3d. The registered debt, on the 30th April 1814, amounted to rupees 21,31,92,502.

4th. The registered debt, on the 30th April 1821, amounted to rupees 25,85,06,549.

5th. The average of annual supplies from India to England, (beyond those from England to India) during the 20 years preceding 1813-14, amounted to rupees 38,83,465.

6th. The average annual supply (similarly measured), from India to England, during the eight years, from 30th of April 1814, to 30th April 1822, amounted to rupees 1,05,90,515.

7th. The cash balances of the three Presidencies, on the 30th April 1814, amounted to rupees 4,80,67,149.

8th. The cash balances, on the 30th April 1821, was rupees 9,78,62,227.

Some of the charges of the past year not having been yet finally adjusted, the amount of Bengal surplus cannot be precisely stated; but the revenues having amounted to Rupees 11,39,37,580, if we assume the charges of the sum anticipated in the regular estimate, *viz.*—Rupees 9,08,04,785, the probable surplus may be calculated at Rupees 2,31,32,795.

It is proper to explain, that in extending the account of the supplies to England, to the end of 1821-22, we have been obliged, in the absence of the Bombay accounts, to take as an estimate, the amount furnished from that Presidency in the past year. The average, however, of the past eight years in the general account of the three Presidencies, can be little affected by any difference in the statements of estimated and actual disbursements at Bombay.

We have the honour, &c.

(Signed) HOLT MACKENZIE,
Secretary to Gov. Rev. Dept.

J. W. SHERER,
Accountant General.

(A true copy) HASTINGS.